Praise for *Salvage List*

"With tender elegance, and a clear, frank eye and voice, Chera Hammons in *Salvage List* explores 'the many ways to be alive.' These richly endearing poems glimmer with multiple windows and doors—changing seasons, relationship with illness, running mares, yucca plants. They feel like instant friends."

—Naomi Shihab Nye

"Chera Hammons' *Salvage List* is ripe with myriad nests: cabbage moths practicing autosarcophagy in preparation for flight, a hatchery of rainbow trout, condominiums constructed by blue wasps to imprison soon-to-be-devoured orb weavers, a grandmother's flashy woven wool coat, a baby cottontail's nest, and finally, as all true children of the Texas Panhandle know, Mason jars, for putting food by. Yet of all of these sequences of nested miracles, the one that strikes this reader the sharpest is the series including 'Chupacabra,' 'The Making of the Horse,' 'Mustang,' 'Red Mare,' and 'Trespasses.' For it is these that illustrate Hammons' wisdom (and the wisdom of all poets), that 'now we are strung together of mismatched pieces, / and those who bore us bestow us with our names / as another once named / what had been found in a garden, all those teeming wild and baffled beasts,' that we might nest within our shared and gorgeous tongues."

—Gary Worth Moody, author of *The Burnings*, co-winner
of the New Mexico / Arizona Book Award in Poetry

"It's said that the oldest souls are those who agree to shoulder heaps of trauma in their next life, ailing in body or spirit, walking among us as wounded healers. In Chera Hammons' breathtaking new collection, *Salvage List*, it's the body that ails amid a prickly landscape of locoweed, yucca spikes, and land hurricanes in the Texas Panhandle. Although illness walks beside her in the supermarket and they argue as couples do, although she knows the inhospitable earth will swallow the aching bones of her old horses and donkeys as well as her own, there is always mercy. There is the unspoken bargain with the barren land and its feral shadows: let us abide together in a semblance of healing and survival, saying, 'I am broken, choose me.' As we all are. As we all must, finally, choose what to salvage of our own woundedness in this wild, drought-hardened world that we love despite ourselves."

—Linda Parsons, author of *Valediction: Poems and Prose*

Salvage List

Fort Smith, Arkansas

poems

Salvage List

Chera Hammons

SALVAGE LIST

Cover image: Prickly Pear Cactus, Getty Images via Canva Pro License

Author photo: Daniel Miller

Edited by Casie Dodd
Design & typography by Belle Point Press

Belle Point Press, LLC
Fort Smith, Arkansas
bellepointpress.com
editor@bellepointpress.com

Find Belle Point Press
on Facebook, Substack,
and Instagram (@bellepointpress)

Printed in the United States of America

29 28 27 26 25   1 2 3 4 5

Library of Congress Control Number: 2025936156

ISBN: 978-1-960215-40-6

SALV/BPP47

To Daniel

Contents

iii.

AUTHOR'S NOTE

The first diagnosis I received that made any sense was Lyme disease. I had most of the symptoms. Blood tests revealed that I had been exposed to the *Borrelia burgdorferi* bacteria. I had often walked through fields and woods, heedless of any danger. A long time before, I had written in a journal about having a circular rash on my thigh, painless but large, in gradients of red. I had worried it was a spider bite. Eventually, it had faded. It faded from memory, too. But I clearly remembered the onset of Lyme symptoms when I was around sixteen years old. They had hit me like a brick wall: fever, nausea, dizziness so severe I could sometimes barely stand. Terrible arthritis in my hips, hands, and knees. Confusion and suicidal ideations.

Over years of Lyme treatments, some of my symptoms improved or disappeared. There were no more unpredictable bouts of pneumonia, no more dangerous fevers. I no longer got lost on the way home. But other symptoms got worse—neck pain, migraines, fatigue, rapid heart rate, brain fog, joint pain, allergies to foods and fragrances. I started to think Lyme disease might only be part of the puzzle.

Around the time of the 2019–2020 pandemic, as the world as we knew it changed irrevocably, I learned that I also have a genetic connective tissue disorder. I told my doctor about how I used to dislocate my shoulder sometimes as a preteen working around horses, how I'd learned to hit it against the barn wall to get it back into socket. Her eyes widened, and that's when I learned that some of the experiences I'd always taken for granted weren't normal.

Meanwhile, finding myself suddenly unemployed and uninsured, stuck at home, and utterly burned out on both writing and teaching, I decided to research my genealogy. For the first time in my life, I felt directionless, and it seemed like knowing where I came from might help me determine where to go next.

Lineage on my father's side had already been well documented: mostly Belgian, French, and English immigrants escaping religious persecution; one of them was credited with bringing the Hollyhock flower to America, a lovely legacy. But my mother had been orphaned when she was four years old and spent much of her childhood in foster homes, and though she had several brothers and sisters, no one had yet attempted to trace their genealogy.

I went into a deep dive of birth and death certificates. We seemed prone, on my mother's side, to sudden and brutal accidents. Especially the men. One of my great-great-grandfathers, in the early 1900s, had died when his automobile got stuck on a train track. Another had been a machinist working on some equipment atop a building. While drunk, he fell off the building and somehow severed his arm on the way down. He survived the fall but succumbed to blood loss and infection. It had never been a secret that alcoholism was in our genes, but where it started is impossible to guess.

Farther back, there had been an early governor of North Carolina, and a priest who died of illness at sea on the way back to England to visit his relatives. One of my ancestors had been third in line to the throne after Mary, Queen of Scots. To the alarm of my cats, after discovering this, I tried to learn to play the bagpipes. My only excuse is that we all did things during the pandemic that we regret.

There was not much information about the women in my mother's family, who had been mostly seamstresses and farm wives, until I got to Rebecca Nurse.

The name sounded familiar. When I Googled her, I found out why. She had been hanged at Salem for being a witch, accused by neighbors who were at least partially motivated to do so out of jealousy over her elevated position in the community and her prized herd of pigs. I imagined the trauma of her children, who had seen their mother put to death for the sake of nothing more than envy, rumor, and hysteria. I wondered how much of their memory was housed in my own cells through routes of generational trauma. I thought of my own traumas, physical and emotional: the sicknesses and injuries, the misunderstandings, the previous abusive marriage.

Meanwhile, when I remembered to look up from my research and glance around me, the world was still slowly spinning. We were somehow at both our best and our worst. The animals were coming back to their old habitats.

The polluted waters were clearing. People were doing kind things for each other. There were also morgue trucks parked outside hospitals, talks of triage. There was still selfishness and intolerance and violence and fear. I thought a lot those days about how a doctor might choose who to treat. I thought about what mercy means to different people. I was fascinated by what people tried to hold onto to make this new reality tolerable. It seemed so random. Rare houseplants. Cat litter. Toilet paper.

Everything became so distilled. People reevaluated their jobs, their connections. The way they spent their limited time on earth. I thought a great deal about what we try to save, as opposed to how much we are actually capable of saving.

Salvage List, which consists of poems written predominantly between 2017 and 2021, comes from the intersection where all of those considerations meet: what we inherit and what we leave behind us. What we can control and what we can't. The way we learn to inhabit our failing bodies in a failing world. The sorts of lifelines we grasp in order to keep ourselves from drowning. What kindness really means. What it means to have agency over the lives of others and over the lives of animals.

Salvage List is my journey to come to terms with all that has formed me. To understand it. On the way, I discovered how much history is remembered within my body, and marveled at it.

If I have learned anything, it is that none of us should be here. So much went into making each one of us, so much tragedy and joy, so many decisions and catastrophes, so much chance. So many contradictions and complexities. So much had to happen. If just one thing had been different, maybe . . . Maybe . . . And yet, we're here, and we're so much more than the sum of our parts.

I hope you will leave *Salvage List* wanting to solve your own mysteries. I hope this book helps you discover for yourself the things you believe are worth keeping. But mostly, I hope it reminds you to keep going forward as long as you can, knowing even as the world falls to pieces around you, that you're surrounded by the miraculous.

i.

Anything Worth Saving

They say the body can remember feeling pain,
but not well enough to feel it twice.
Once it has passed, it has gone for good.
See the way a person curls around an ache;
later, try to prove that it was there.
Ask a mother who has untangled her blood from her child's
if she would do it all over again.

Outside these walls, the troubled world is waiting.
I want more than just to survive.
I want something I don't know how to name.
In the obstetrician's office, pictures of flowers
litter the walls. Labeled *pistil, stamen, petal*.
People listen to music while they wait.
In farther rooms, faded cotton gowns
are folded. Meant to be tied in the front.

They say to be cursed, you've got to believe in curses.
What is a woman, then? Can you kiss
any of that hurt away?
The wood is too green and will not burn.
We leave with what we carried when we arrived—
a hunger, a love of air. That's it.
I don't know how to take compliments,
so I bury them alive.

You know how when you look at a light for too long,
everything gets the shape of that brightness on it.
People ask, this thing that you made.
Did you have to make it? Does it have meaning?
Did you have to do it so that you could live?

Some days, you have to forget pain
before you can make yourself believe
that this world is anything worth saving.

Now there are scars where the wounds have been,
the same shape as the wounds.
Now we are ruining our bodies again
and trusting that they will forgive us.

Trace Elements

I like to think that I was asked,
Who wants this body? and I did.
That when I stepped within its boundaries,
it still gleamed, smooth and unblemished
as a tumbled stone. It had been
prepared for me. I didn't know what flaws
to look out for. It was my first time in a body.

In the bright world, the world that this skin breaches into,
the body is an animal that wants.
Any animal that hungers is one that fears.
So I feed it, but its hunger keeps returning.

Here is a person in a cage of bones.
Here are bones wrapped in spools of flesh.
Here is a life that is made of water
but is not a part of the sky or the sea.
When I try not to think of the illness,
I think only of the illness.

Here is the point of no coming back.
Here is a shipwreck in a bottle.
The empty mast has broken,
snapped over in some gray storm.
The bowsprit is a briny woman carved of wood.

Here is an hour spent drawing vials of blood,
labeled with a name that my father provided.
Here is a meander through ashy trees,
my legs against the warm damp ribs of a horse.

I have outlived both Jesus and Sylvia Plath.
Salt seasons this body and preserves it.
I like to think that I will be asked,
Are you ready?, and that
I will know the answer.

Imago

To form wings, caterpillars must digest
parts of themselves in the closet of their darkness.

We live so many lives, even we can't keep
track of them all. Take this worn-out soul,

which has moved from girlhood
to womanhood like a trout surfacing

in the light, a flicker of mouth,
then disappearing again into a shadowed bed.

It has been married and divorced
and remarried.

It has prayed and blasphemed in equal measure
to see which one worked.

It has read books and written them;
some of both, it has abandoned.

It has spoken and then taken the words
back into its teeth and swallowed them.

Even as our bodies unspool from their frames,
we are always only *becoming*.

I don't remember home well enough to get back,
so this place becomes a home.

It is summer. The cabbage worms
have broken through their skin to inhabit the sky.

That's the kind of revision we long for, the kind
some religions call heaven.

A Daughter Learns to Fish

The sign said the fish were guaranteed to bite.
When her father helped her reel the line in,

the pole leapt and bowed, and a rainbow trout breached
at the end of a filament as unyielding as a prophecy.

Her mother helped her to hold up the fish and said,
If only we had remembered the camera.

It was the most slippery and the most holy object
the girl had ever seen.

It was like holding a sunset surrounded by silver,
the shimmer and goosebump of a change,

the *not-knowing-what-will-happen*,
which, once lost, might never be rediscovered.

She cried for miles when they left.
Not because of leaving the fish in Colorado,

though they had had to leave it.
But because for the first time

she had held in her hands her own
small and bright horizon.

Texas Strong

Lines written after a school shooting.

My mother used to say
that seeing blue dragonflies
means it will rain soon.
I still haven't lived long enough
to know if it's true.
I might never live long enough.

Every August, blue wasps make houses of mud
mouthful by mouthful, building temples
for petrified orb weavers,
preserving them alive for months
until the day they are devoured.

It's September already, I tell everyone I see,
as if we all fell asleep driving here,
and if you believe in an afterlife,
you must believe in waking up somewhere different,
a different version of yourself.

Everywhere I look, there's
the shell of a bullet.
Where did the summer go?
Nowhere. It just goes.

You will miss not knowing how the world ends.
There are so many times you will think, *This is it*.
But it won't be yet. Then maybe it will.

We wait in rooms that might still one day
open to the sun.

The dragonflies are seaglass blue,
which may mean everything or nothing at all.

At surprising times, you learn again
how there has always been
some hurt you won't suffer,
and some other hurt you will.

My Grandmother Hated Grackles

My grandmother's garden would abide no sinner
but the green-shined birds
that burgled peanuts from the jays.

They were trash birds, she used to say.
Worthless, dirty, diseased, and mited.
Bullies to other birds.

Before the estate sale, my mother said,
Take anything you want from the closets.

So I picked a woven wool coat
that was brilliant and strange,
the sort of whimsy my stern grandmother
had never worn once in her life.

It didn't remind me of her at all.
My mother said, *I'm surprised you picked that.*

The last time I ever saw my grandmother,
she asked the nurse who I was,
and the nurse said, *That's your granddaughter.*

She studied my features, younger version of her own.
I saw her recognize herself and become afraid
before she declared she didn't know me
and turned her face to the eggshell wall.

When I was a little girl, before anything had ever happened,
I crouched in her garden and picked unripe tomatoes,
admiring how they were just starting to blush with sun.

I never confessed to this.
But now and then, I catch my grandmother again
in glimpses, and she knows.

She even forgives, now, some of these transgressions,
though her coat waits in my untidy closet
like nothing else I own.

What the Genetic Counselor Says

Your body is an inheritance
of certainty and uncertainty
strung together like baroque pearls,
crooked from growing to fit oddly shaped places,
but so luminous that they are desired, loved.

I know everyone had plans for you.
I think, *I had plans for myself.*

After the appointment, I ask my mother
questions about family history and health,
and she remembers more and more
that might mean something:

My father's fallen arches,
which kept him from the army.
Her double-jointed fingers.
The back pain she had thought came
from having been hit with a belt in foster care,
the lick of that cold metal buckle
its own kind of guarantee:
the suspicion that everyone but her
deserves mercy.

Generations of knee surgery at young ages.
Chronically upset stomachs,
chronically faulty hearts.
I am the only one who wants to know why.

My mother has told me often before,
I think you'd feel better if you'd pray.
Prayer: another glistening
ordered line.

I try to remember that every heirloom once
had reason to be new.

But now we are strung together of mismatched pieces,
and those who bore us bestow us with our names
as another once named
what had been found in a garden,
all those teeming wild and baffled beasts.

After Tracing My Genealogy
to Rebecca Nurse

Now I know why we've carried so long
this vision of the earth falling away
to leave us swinging through the loud void,

not like stars riding the pendulum through dark matter—
an emptiness that fills with song—

but like the childless swing in the playground
creaking as the wind meets the chains.

I hear it. My mother hears it. It is our inheritance.

It is mine as much as the scar on my knee
from falling on glass when I was a child is mine.
The injury that left a triangle of thickened skin,
and the blood that was more vivid than the pain.

Years ago, but not so long ago, really,
we buried two horses in the pasture:
a liver chestnut whose heart had given out,
the way my father's father's heart had.
A blood bay that had succumbed to cancer,
like mother's mother did.

Now the living horses sleep over the graves
with lowered heads, as though they hear
whickering underneath.

But it is only the sigh of the earth
as it settles to fill gaps between the smoothed white bones.
The earth will swallow these horses one day, too.

It will swallow me and all that I hold dear.
Is this mercy? Maybe there has never been mercy.

Maybe there has only been a father who learned
of his own helplessness too soon.

Maybe there has been a mother who herself
wanted only to be loved.

The Moon of a Moon is a Moonmoon

This is the algebra of language: wordmath.
Try it. An ebb and flow of sweetness: honeymoon.
Childhood: the head covering of someone
who is still discovering what to forget.
The friend of my friend is my friendfriend.

Sorry, bad example; the second *friend* is silent.
There but not there. Something implied, imagined.
Like how I once told students
Kill your darlings! But don't bury them.
And somehow they knew that what I meant
is that redundancy can be as efficient as resurrection.
Though there was no real danger; we killed nothing.

When the moon appears in a lake,
it means it has dropped low enough for you to wade into.
If you want. The moon is blank as a mirror.
It doesn't mind if you reflect in its reflection.

Foreshadowing: darkness that walks in front of you.
Slumlord: the god of not-enough.

If you are male, you are man, you are he,
I am *fe*. I am *wo*. I am *s*.
The plural and the possessive. The hiss
of air escaping from a tire. Tired.

Think about this: the enemy of my friend
could still be my friend,
but probably isn't.

Is there any better way to say
that one can orbit a body that orbits another body?
That gravity ties us to each other?
And that other bodies orbit us?

—No, it seems we have finally run out of words.
Removing the spaces between them
is the only way to make something new.

I am the daughter of my father;
I am the daughter of my mother, too.

How to Get a Hoya to Bloom

We have carried this single dream through a long winter
of silences. Carried this green thumb
and the greening hands and the safety of being indoors.
Carried the turn of hands,
and the leafless runner that goes farther and farther
into empty space, seeking something in the air it can root in.

The warmth of sun withdraws with the light
and draws the plant with which it has married.
Carries it in a riptide of bright
though it must stop at the glass
which it doesn't possess the strength to break,
though the runners press hard, hard
against clarified and transparent sand.

And the arms spread as wide as they can get
in a room this size. Most people will wrap the runners
around the soil of the pot they sprang from
and weigh them down with rocks
before such unsightliness as has been allowed here.

Isn't flowering what it was meant to do? Not only this.
This strange house, full of runners reaching, nothing else.
The green immigrant leaves, the tendrils
that yearn for belonging.

There are two options, I read, and only two.

The first: Withhold water from it for five weeks in spring.
A plant that believes it is dying will focus on flowering.
And for such temerity its reward will be its relief,
distilled water cold from the tank under the sink,
drawn from the dark underground pool of mineral
below us. Just in time.

The second: Let it be the single green dream
in a room of forgetfulness.
Every language is one that can be lost.
The world forgets even the names of its gods
unless they have been excavated and peer-reviewed.

And the cold still pool in the dark magnetic earth
is forgotten, too, again and again,
though it gives more of itself for each mercy.

Monstera deliciosa

There are histories everywhere that are there
but silent. Every day since the monstera arrived,
there has been a finger pushed into the soil
knuckle deep, the early-opened curtains,
the gentle mist from the spray bottle,

the precise rotation in front of a northern window
while I think of tropical plants I had before
that did not live. The window that I had before.

This bright one not at all like that other one,
in that cold dim house, that small dark room,
the dying globe willow waiting outside there
bowed like a weeping woman
while wasps drank the sap from its wounds.
It cried out but no one heard it.
Its mooncast shadow pressed itself against the glass.

No matter now; I survived it.
And the monstera ripples with health.
Daily it consumes a little more of its corner.
Each new leaf becomes more fenestrated
than the last, until the upper leaves
are so filled with holes
that the light reaches all the parts of itself
that came before.

Fenestration, like the French
word for window: *fenêtre.*
Or, if you go back far enough in time,
fenestre. As if the roof in the word
has a snake hiding in its rafters.

These smaller, lovelier lives
move softly through the wake of mine.
The burdens which are chosen,
so much easier to manage
than any other kind.

The Fall of Rome

The city's women knew too well
that when the seasons changed,
a house must change, too.

In the last days of the democracy
they walked barefoot through the rooms,
shaking the dust out of the sun-faded curtains,
watching for the scorpions
which sometimes crept along the walls
in autumn's early chill.

They swept, as was their habit. They polished.
They put heavier quilts upon the beds.
They watered the houseplants
which were not yet dormant,
aware that even the hardy pothos
would not long outlive any woman
who had stood in the stead of rain.

That spring, when the newly unfurled leaves had draped
tender and neon on stems that reached
from the dark green center mass,
that sudden color had been so vivid
that it hurt something vital
they thought they had lost,
so that they felt the loss of it again.
A final flare of sunset. The blue jay feathers

they'd gathered as girls,
which must have wound up in boxes in attics,
going to dust and mites.
Those feathers had been almost fluorescent
against the brown winter grass.

They had long known that safety was the same
as that bright blue: just a trick of the light.
Some lies, so perfect, so precise,
you'd do almost anything to forgive them.

Bathsheba in Church

Men in dark suits will tell you
how to speak of the world's sins,

how to feel the spasms of your own misunderstandings.
This pain isn't punishment, they tell you. *It's love.*

They will lead you in songs of praise.
They will tell you that everything you lose

is because you were meant for something better.
But no one will tell you what to call the wound

that spreads soft as roses in your chest
while your heart cries in alarm,

panicked by its nearness.
No one will tell you how to go on living

once you have become the vessel
to collect all of a person's carelessness.

I didn't know if it was a secret violence.
I didn't know if the wound was only mine.

I sat with knees touching
and legs crossed at the ankles

while I learned that I had been lost, then found,
lost, then found, over and over again, like a memory.

Finally I asked my mother why
she had never told me about this kind of hurt,

and she said, surprised, *I thought
it only belonged to me.*

Tree Stand

I shivered in the extra camouflage jacket that a man
I hadn't stopped loving yet had found in the farmhouse closet

after he'd awakened me in darkness, chilly,
when I was empty with hunger,

before we drove down a shrinking road
and got out to walk through trees so dark

I could only follow him. Looming
above us in branches, the wooden ledge.

The ladder's metal rungs, so cold they hurt.
The borrowed jacket smelled of must

and want. It smelled of his father's stale sweat.
The morning light paled in blue gradients.

A sparrow darted between the branches
close enough that I felt the breath of its wings,

and a peregrine pursued it, intention
full of silence, like the trails through this wilderness.

The wooden boards creaked if I moved at all.
When a doe stepped from the thicket

I lowered my eyes, covered my ears,
uncertain whether he would spare it.

He had never spared anything before.
Beside me he raised the rifle. Steady this time.

I imagined, if he hit the doe, how I would run
to it and kneel there, pressing my hands

to hold in the bitten-in-two red heart
as it spilled our terrible betrayal

into the unforgiving ground, and tell it
I bore witness to this. I will mourn you.

ii.

It Gets Easier

I see what looks like trouble,
something that doesn't fit,

a writhing and twisting
near the new-leafed tree

as if two bare branches have fallen but live
their own lives under some dark curse.

What I find is a braid of two snakes
knotting and unknotting

their bodies, heads coral
like the flesh of an unripe peach

and slim cold muscle sliding,
skin countershaded to look

like double-braided rawhide.
Two coachwhips, oblivious

to the world and me.
I have seen single snakes

periscoping from the tall grass
but never two together like this.

So this is where their kind begins.
Somehow, I had never asked this question.

When they untie they fly away over the ground
like ribbons driven by the wind.

Let us tie a knot into the day;
let's see if the love will stay this time.

I saw what looked like fear
but it was a wreath of beauty,

not disaster. Time heals everything,
everything, I believe it. Every wound

(except a mortal one).

When the Cottontail Doesn't Return

In a fur-lined nest under wreaths of lamb's ears,
an unmoving rabbit kit shrinks into bone,

having given up hours ago. The kit I take from the dog
that has discovered the nest suffers. I tell my husband

it would be quicker to let the dog keep it.
By quicker, I mean the measure of the young heart's hurt.

I don't mean to sound so harsh.
The kit I find huddled against the house,

eyes sealed shut, trembling, might yet be saved.
Tell me what sort of world this is:

to move into light for the first time
and find it contains the devouring mouth.

Not knowing that there can ever be more than this.
Then the strange, unsteady lift, the glass dropper

of unfamiliar milk pressed against the gums,
the voice, like those it will fear one day, saying "Live."

And again I ask: "What could this mean?"
And hope the answer is something remarkable.

These Habits

Every morning, the coyote passes through
the land that I have called my home,
slips under the pasture fence
and trots northeast toward the canyon,
hidden inside the arroyo.

The coyote's path was worn when I came here
and still is, as if my human life
has made no impression on this place.
She doesn't go around me.

At first, I laughed at her audacity.
Then I started every day to watch for her.

She comes from across the road,
hesitates, reads the wind in both directions
and casts her question like a water-witcher.

I have seen her flatten into invisibility
when cars pass. I have seen her snap soundlessly
at flies. She pants. The rough roll of her winter coat
hangs at her hips as she sheds,
as if she wears a half-discarded cloak.

She is there, and then she vanishes,
and there isn't any proof she stood
so long in the ironweed weighing her risk.

She doesn't make mistakes.
Once she is satisfied with her loneliness,
the way she slides under the fence is a breath out.

She leaves tufts of hair in the yuccas
like mementos for a lover to keep.
The hair is coarser than a horse's on my palm.

There is a secret between us.
Her silence betrays it:

how it means she knows that I am near.
She knows that I'm her danger.

Mercy

While riding two strong Icelandic horses,
we come across a doe and fawn
in a deep green meadow and fall silent.

The deer don't fear us
since we have borrowed
these other, gentler bodies.

How long we stand watching them,
not wanting this respite to end,
while our mares worry their bits
and shift their restless weight beneath us.

Maybe the fawn will grow
antlers like the spread of a canopy;
he will learn to carry himself soundlessly
as he flees through the thickest trees.

Maybe the doe won't suffer
too much in the end.

Who can say whether the meadow
will remain a meadow?

The morning's birdsong breaks
into the protest of flight,
and the deer are gone.

We have only rented the horses
for an hour or two;
there is never enough time here.

We don't talk about how one day,
someone will look at these mares,
grown arthritic and thin,
and think of the importance

of a place in the skull,
above and between
those dark adored eyes.

And how quietly we can carry
such knowledge as this with us,
taking the ending of horses along
no matter where we go,

as though this is not a burden
almost as alarming to contain
as the love that is the reason for it.

And how strongly we still feel sometimes
that we have been kind enough to each other,
in this one life—that we could ever
be kind enough.

Bound

In the shade of the stunted hackberry tree,
two donkeys, one young, one old,
groom each other's backs,
the teeth of each one scraping gently
against the lay of the other's coat,
a utility of tenderness.

It is said that one donkey can hear another bray
up to sixty miles away in the desert.
That is how they discover each other
in that undulating wilderness:
by sending their strange music
into the lonesome wind
and following the answer.

They need each other,
though they must know
what this need means.

It is said that, where there are two
donkeys, when one dies,
the other will soon follow it.

This is not a kind of romance, but a science:
the body of the animal that is left behind
believes that it is starving,
and its organs fail.

It seems like either courage or absurdity
for beasts of burden to love like this,
in a way that must ruin one of them,
but they do it stoically, without assumption.

And if you own a donkey, what can you do
but find a companion for it,
though knowing where this will lead?

One that is lonely will keep you up at night,
sending its sorrow out again and again
into the consuming darkness,

which never answers,
and that is worse.

Why We Had No Use for a Rooster,
and What That Drove Us to Do

He entered the morning
unashamed, as so many male animals do.
He soon convinced us of his disregard
of all our careful planning
in proud syllables like coos and tiny trumpets.
We had loved him like a hen,
fed him mushy grapes, watched him grow magnificent.
Too magnificent. He shone with dark gold,
brown, and green, the bright red of his comb
a darted wound, tail like a solar flare.

We ignored the problem until we couldn't,
those once tentative crows
expanding soon to fill each morning,
swelling one clear verse after another,
opposing neighborhood restrictions,
until he sang half an hour at a time with wonderful skill.
I spent my days Googling ways
to keep a rooster from crowing, reading stories
of birds strangled slowly to death
by silencing collars that looked like fancy bowties.

Finally, from the pet carrier in the back seat:
quiet. He nestled into an old white towel,
pleased with his dominion,
rubbing his beak on his flintspecked wing.

We gave him away like a veiled bride.
We knew better than to ask what would happen to him.
I wanted to ask, *Is this enough?*
Could I ever make amends?

Whatever happens, may it be painless and clean,
we begged in silence,
wanting only what we couldn't do ourselves.

Stray

We dig a tabby kitten from the undercarriage
of our beat-up farm truck where, to our best guess,

it has been crying since its abandonment
hours ago in darkness.

Now its new claws clutch
through the knit of my shirt to my skin.

Now the owner's problem is ours.
The tiny body hums. I once read that,

even during vivisections, dogs kept
wagging their tails, licked the hands

that held the scalpels while
their exposed hearts thrummed.

I couldn't read any more. This is the mystery—
that a heart could spend time in our sterile rooms

and still believe that there is good in us.
It's never going to be enough,

all this talk about what mercy is.
What kind of loss would be the least.

Feral Cat

Nomad
in the vastness of brick houses

Every slant of light
is a bed

I can guess what she hasn't seen yet
of cruelty

but this knowledge
does not improve me

Another bright hour
is before her

drifting
between what she is
and what she will be

like a delicate white veil
that is riven,

at times,
with songbirds

Cat Goddess

Should I take this golden-eyed worship
as miracle or omen? Who would belie
such soft-stomached contentment?
I am meant for something. I am something to them.
Whatever room I enter, they gather at my feet,
thrumming, bags of organ, muscle, bone.
Be still. We are as safe as I can make us.
I don't tell them I could afford to lose this comfort
more than many others.

I am not a mother, but I could be,
could have been. Or is it a sort of baptism—
once mother, always mother, no matter how brief?
Like the summer spider that counter-balances
its web with stones, I am anchored
to an earth that sways,
and my hope is held in place by the swaying.
My home, the center where I dream.
I repair the threads where burdens tear through.
Who could call a woman the weaker vessel?
We know how to carry anything.

Now I am stockpiling my prescriptions,
halving them, or skipping them,
refilling them as often as I am allowed.
Every therapy is experimental.
Country, will you let me vanish

slowly, piece by piece?
These aching feet. To warm them
with sweet and easy affection, whatever I can afford.
Come to me, my dears. My beauties.

Some say that love has no fear in it.
That can't be true, because if it is,
no one has ever loved.

Some Days, the Pain Medication Doesn't Work

Someone speaks from a room that muffles voices;
this house contains too much furniture for meaning.

The news is a droning despair, like the mud hornet
hitting the smudged window over and over, a clumsy

incantation. Sound bites that tell of the urge to survive.
I try not to spill coffee when I hold the shaking cup

against my lower lip. I keep
my anger taped up like a package

so I do not spill the crumbs as I carry it.
I curl in like these arthritic fingers,

which bear twisted silver rings. The mud hornet
will give up and I will never find it again,

not even when I sweep the dusty corners later.
I only notice its absence because of the quiet.

No words are the right words for this.
I leave the thesaurus open to *body*.

Dear Disease

Before I knew it, I was living in rooms with you
like you were the partner I had chosen.
And every decision was Ours.
What should we do today?
What should we wear? you ask.
I wear my jacket collar up to block the wind.
You walk beside me, rubber-soled,
to the supermarket, where you take out of the basket
what I put in. Aren't you a fine dictator of appetites.
We sit on the couch and flip through the channels,
a rolodex of noise and want.
We argue as every couple might,
until I know what you will say
even before you say it.
Shut up, just shut up, I want to tell you,
but I am too polite, and you always get your way.
In the mornings, I wake up with you.
You are in the mirror, framed over spit in the sink,
looking back at me expectantly.
Everywhere I look, in fact, there you are waiting,
impenetrable, inescapable, a dome of demands.
I abide. Do you hear me? I am still here.
I am ringing against
this prison's walls with one note,
like the heart of a bell.

An Abecedarian for Barrenness

At first, the thought of being lonely didn't
bother me; after all, the world already has its share of

children. And there is no good reason to mete out a
disease like mine. I will not contain more than my own death.

Every morning, lines of blackbirds rise
from the sumacs in the canyon and enter the most

golden hours of their days, while red-tailed
hawks hunt the birds that fall behind.

In the evenings, I peel pomegranates, the heart-red
juice staining my thumbnail. One taste of fruit can

keep someone from paradise, so I'm careful.
Light falls in slats on the floor beneath the windows; it

moves with the earth's turning, and then it's gone. I will leave
nothing behind me here but waste and

offal, bone, knuckled worry, forgotten words, the
peel of what I have consumed to live. Through the

quiet of the starsick night, I sometimes
realize I am the ghost that haunts this house, my own

sighing is the cold draft under the doors,
the blur in the back of every mirror is me.

Under dark trees, the waiting deer are luminous spirits shedding
velvet antlers. I can ask a machine anything, so I ask it

What is the range of honeybees? Miles away, bees are singing of the
xeric flowers of my yard, thorny sweetness dragged by heaven's

yellow eye. Could I want what burns and unsights me? Could we, unwitting
zealots, call such startling indifference God?

Ghazal after the Electrocardiogram

With the cold nodes stuck to my skin, I lie holding the thin sheet to my
bare chest
and hoping my heart is not defective, though I know I've seen it break

a thousand times. No one speaks but the machine. Like the earth, I'm
measured
in mountains. I am weighed in water, my body a shore where mysterious
waves break

and vanish. Needles. Nausea and electricity. I grow sea legs. My brother once
told me
If you're that sick, die. I imagined the railroad crossing by his house, how
it'd be to not brake

at those flashing red lights. I don't know how I can want to live and die
at the same time,
the prescription bottles on my counter like little prayers, like firebreaks

during a dry year. I don't remember the first time I told someone I loved them,
or who it was. I remember watching the bloom of summer daybreak

from the back of a fiery red dun mare that died a long time ago.
She ran at the neighbor's fence one windy day and broke

her neck. I thought if I could get her to stand again, she would live, though her body was too heavy for me to lift. A broken horse can't be unbroken.

But it can forget. The doctors have the results. We graph like earthquakes. The sound in the shaking. The disarrangement when a line breaks.

The Doctor Says to Make My Body into an Unfriendly Place

The doctor says *Sugar feeds illness*.
It's just such easy energy.
You're a walking Petri dish and agar,
born to make bacteria thrive.
Starve them instead.

No sugar, no gluten, no dairy,
no soy, no nightshades, no corn,
no onions, no garlic, no figs or potatoes.

A diet becomes a survey
of what I used to enjoy.
When I think of eating, it's with longing,
as if I haven't had a good meal
since childhood. As if it's
a former indulgence,
grown out of.

I inherited most of my yearnings.
When I tell my mother we are descended
from a matriarch hanged at Salem,
she laughs and says, *I'm glad we were the witches
and not the ones doing the hanging*.
I post pictures of my late grandmother,
and Facebook wants to tag her face as mine.

The doctor can't tell me whether
I am starving the illness
more than I am myself.
She can't tell me if this hunger
belongs to me or to the disease.

At least I am the ending of it.
At least I leave with what I brought.

But ask me for forgiveness, body. Try.
If you ask it, I could forgive anything.

Grocery Delivery

It must be an intimate thing,
to choose a pear
for someone else.

To thumb the soft curve
of a peach you won't keep,
taking care not to slip
a fingernail
through the skin.

I hope the shopper
who stands in my stead
is happy when she wakes up
after a good night's sleep.

I hope she has never been sick
a day in her life.
That she has never
been stuck fast somewhere.

I hope she is unable to resist
the heirloom tomatoes,
and lifts them to breathe the sharp
exotic scent of vine,
though they are too expensive
and I never buy them.

I hope she is the sort of person
who sometimes spends too much
on a tomato.

I imagine her pressing
the dusky avocados, thinking
what we would both know to be true:
This one needs more time.

I imagine how she must knock
on the watermelons
and listen for a difference,
the way I used to do,
longing for a *yes.*

35 mm

The semesters I studied photography,
I would step into the college darkroom
and listen to see if I was alone,
and it seemed my question kept going
and never returned,
lost in a darkness I couldn't see the end of
while I waited in the sweetness between disasters.

Housed in a close closet off the lightless hallway,
I loaded exposed film onto the reel
in darkness so thorough
I forgot that my eyes were open.

My hands had memorized where the film canister lay
on the table, the scissors, reel, bottle opener,
developing container, lid and funnel.
That smooth cylinder, palm long, kept its secrets
until I asked for them:
gray images of trapped souls.
Fountains in everlastingly flowered parks.
An old dog that would never give up on living.

There was no time and so much time,
it was hard not to think of all that had been lost.
I stood in the darkness listening to myself breathe
while the film whispered, unspooling and re-spooling,
like the hours. Later, still in darkness,
silver halides moved to show the shape
each frame of light had taken.
I held the container that held a record
of fractions of seconds of brilliance
that had been multiplied.

I worry, sometimes, that the answer came back,
but I had already given up waiting for it.

Driving through a Freezing Fog

As I move, the world moves with me,
and I am alone within a wall of cloud,
surrounded like a storm's eye.

Here is a boundary, and there
is a boundary, the boundary is a ring,
and beyond the boundary, noise:

wind that comes from nowhere
and goes nowhere,
birdsong without a bird.

Shaggy cows watch me go by
with surprised expressions
they carry the entirety of their brief lives.

Here is the form of a skunk
that has always been dead—
it came into the world that way.

After I pass, the mysterious white veil
swallows the land,
and the land is gone for good.

In the distance, there is a point of light
that separates. Now it is two points.

Now I am alongside it—it is gone.
It was no one, or everyone;

it had its own center.
It will end up who knows where.

There are more lights ahead now,
lines of them, bright and charging
forward. A highway.

You, too, are a light
traveling fast, and you, too,
can refuse to be comforted.

iii.

Vigilance

Because I was watching a line of red ants
I missed the spark that blew behind me,

how orange bloomed then
in wind-whipped petals, open hands of flame.
By the time I noticed it, light leapt
from blade to blade, shriveling the tips

of the drygold brush black.
The hooded man who welded the corner-post
knelt unknowing before an apocalypse,
having too much trusted his fire-watcher.

That was the nearest I have come
to forgetting myself,
not counting all the other times
I've left my body. There would have been
no witnesses this time.

It wasn't too late by the time I realized
I wanted us to make it.
The red ants writhed in the rush
of cold water as they drowned.

Later I realized I had forgotten to shield my sight
from the blue brilliance of the arc—
my eyes, brief wounds I had always suffered,
had learned to hurt.

Two slices of potato, starchy and soothing,
promised transcendence from the pain of the burn,
thick blank coins that closed this vision
while time crawled ahead,
foraging for what it could find.

Doesn't everyone want the sort of currency
that could ferry our losses
through a darkness like this one?

But there is nothing else that can be done.
Our bodies are the only vessels
that could carry them.

Land Management

My husband has cut all of the stalks
off the wild green yuccas and left them where they fell.

Our neighbor has told us this is the only way
to keep those needled fans from spreading;

every inch that a yucca takes up
is an inch that can't be used for grazing.

Already, our fields are filled with spines.
The jenny donkey arms herself with the stalks and carries them,

stems of cut flowers with no container.
When she tires of this, she eats the waxy petals.

She is dark and glossy, not like common gray burros;
the cross on her shoulders hides under her coat.

When we first moved here,
we tried making soap from the yucca root.

We dug up several small ones, asking forgiveness.
The root was white and tough, but it lathered.

Now we dig up yuccas and toss them over the fence to rot.
Now the only yucca we allow to keep its embellishment

is the red one we planted in the flowerbed when we moved in.
This morning, a hummingbird drinks from red blossoms

opened out and emptying their sweetness
to many mouths, like holy vessels.

Killdeer

It fooled me once, when I was a child,
before I understood how much I needed to find
the treasure it guarded in its ring of stones,
needed to imagine holding its black speckled eggs
warm in my hands, sense the life of them
waiting to drink the green air.
Before I needed to believe that a chance
could be miraculous.

When I got too close, that long-ago killdeer
had feigned that it was hurt, fanning its auburn tail
and flapping one wing, then the other,
crying plaintively.
I am broken, it said. *Choose me.*
So I had walked past where the vulnerable
nest must have been
to follow a pleading soul
that always stayed just out of reach
until it lifted into the vast air ahead, unharmed.
I had so wanted, in my girlish heart,
to save it.

Spring mornings now, I still waver
when a killdeer stands and cries
as I walk in the pasture to measure the new grass.
It betrays its own secret, scuttles

ahead of me pretending it is hurt,
though I am no danger to anything it holds dear
and never have been.

But because I chose this
drought-hardened earth,
this pale milk sky,
this wind that sings in the night to no one,
I must follow behind it every time
until it is satisfied.

Locoweed

Growing all winter, certain of itself,
it has waited for the horses to believe in their hunger

enough to try the early green and silver stems
that lie to them about goodness.

It makes itself the only green around.
We have found it out in time

by its early dragonheads of purple flowers.
On our knees as the neighbors drive by,

we pull and pull, getting at the roots.
No one asks what we are doing.

We do it dumbly,
the ground a blur of consequence.

It feels like we are grazing on it ourselves;
our view has become more dirt than sky.

Sometimes when I look up, I can see a paint horse
running on the other side of the canyon,

and know I could never reach it.
Its map of white glints like metal in the morning sun.

This is how I learn that when they point their ears
and study the horizon, my horses

must be watching for other horses.
But who will take up that one's death for it?

Somewhere, there is a mare no one can get to
beating its head against a post.

We pull and pull and pull,
for days at a time, all spring,

not saying how important it is
that our care for one life

means we give up another.
The first time I ever saw one,

I put those flowers to my cheek,
thinking how soft they were. How sweet.

Paradise

On the eighth day, we decided
how to contain our happiness.
That it could fit in the shape of masonry veneer,
repurposed furniture, cars with peeling clearcoats,
a kitchen of organic vegetables.
That we could set it all safely in an unkempt yard
of rosebush, dirt, and sky.

Here we are, then. Taming our land.
Teaching it our will and our caprices.

Look: in the window, an orb weaver
gathers raindrops from her body
with legs that move like a bow across a violin;
she lifts the round jewels of water and drinks.
Though the wind tears her golden thread again and again,
she writes a masterpiece.
Her art is wonderful.

But there is no season of easy survival.
In the summer months this house
is beset by drought and lightning.
Fireflies flash like blessings from the forsythia
and disappear as if they were never there.
Cacti grow rich purple fruit, covered in spines
that make us draw back. The earth is scoured by wind.

Then, the winter, which wraps our walls in stillness, comes,
and we mourn. The trees have been opened.
You can see their secrets on clear cold afternoons,
abandoned nests, broken branches, wounds like ours.

As long as this house stands, perhaps
I can't be banished from our world.
I beg you, say this place is mine. That I own it,
however much I can't belong to it.

Or maybe I belong to nothing.
They tell me my mother was a mountain pine,
roots thrust deep between gray boulders.
My father—so I hear (I never really knew him)—
was moonlight on a river.

Chupacabra

There isn't enough shape remaining
to recognize the dark animal
that shrinks beside the two-lane road,
turned sun-cured leather, drawn tendon,

cracked marrow. It could be a large dog,
a deer, what's left of a calf.
I don't want to call it *monster*,
some myth told and retold until it buries itself,
like our tired human myth,
like the myth of the ground we love.

The cold hangs on like a curse this year,
and the ribby old horses must be blanketed
against the wind's raw throat.
They can't spare the calories it would take to shiver.

The watery sun is lost in a white blanketed sky.
At dawn, the birds stream endlessly
past pale winter stars
and their sadness doesn't have a name.

Today, this body lets me down.
It lets down everyone I know.
One day it will give itself back to the earth,
and then the earth will have to carry it.

Have you loved this place, too, despite its barrenness?
We own what can't be taken from us.

The Making of the Horse

Let this animal bear the collar
of the harness but no collarbone,

an intestine that is unattached to its body wall,
no gallbladder. An esophagus

at right angles, the inability to regurgitate food,
so that indigestion could be its undoing.

May it carry half a ton of body
on four fingernails.

Let it lock its knees to doze,
but require it to dream lying down.

Require it to dream. Ensure that lack of sleep
won't too quickly kill it or those who care for it.

Give it the largest eye, then let it notice
every color but the one it bleeds.

When the animal runs, let it breathe with every stride.
Let it run a long time before it is winded.

Make it lucky enough to want to survive,
generous enough to tolerate mistreatment.

Make it strong enough to carry
the weight of our intentions.

Grant its understanding mostly to gray-haired women
who stand alone in fields, their bodies earthed and steady,

and watch the horizon for signs of bad weather.
Those who know what it is to lose much

and keep going on, though their hearts, too,
could burst with that longing.

Mustang

The desert is a roofless room
where only God can see me.

My arm has become a lariat rope,
uncoiled in the air above a feral animal.

Lariat, from the Spanish *la reatar*, tie again.
It is never enough to tie something once.

I almost don't recognize myself anymore.
The horse circles over the bones of a buried house.

I can touch its breath, but nothing else.
I may not get any closer for months, it's so wary of me.

Before you call me foolish, tell me
you have never wanted to hold a myth.

Tell me you have never loved a morning more
because it held within its brightness the mystery of a night.

Antivenin is made with the poison
it is meant to mend. Like firehawk raptors,

we scatter burning branches over a wild land
that cannot reach us. Set it all aflame.

This place, too, seems too hurt for mending.
Because I care for the horse,

and can never return it to its home,
I can only take its wildness from it.

Gentle it, from the Latin *gentilis*,
which means *of one's own family*.

I must take away its wildness
so that it has enough room for ours.

Red Mare

i.

The red mare believes at first
that she is running away from me,

that it is possible to outrun me.
She runs in sun-baked tracks worn by other horses,

shaking her head in defiance as the fence
without corners turns her and turns her back.

There are half-moons of white in her goldbrown eyes.
She arches her neck. Her coat gleams like a clear sky.

My lunge whip is angled at her hip, but never touches her.
She hasn't realized yet that this is what I want,

to let her run until she starts to think
this flight was never her idea, but mine.

When she grows tired, she will ask
my permission to rest, and I will give it. Soon

now. Soon. Her trust, when it comes,
will seem like witchcraft to someone watching.

Though it will look like giving up,
it is not giving up.

It is the beginning. Red mare, coated in dust, sweat
furring the *V* of her chest, her neck.

As long as she orbits, I am gravity. We sway
each other. The drumming of her hooves—

how it rumbles beneath the soles of my feet,
shakes the ground, settles in my stomach, then my heart.

My heart—until this canter is what keeps me alive.
We both know what it is to approach an afterlife,

see it narrowing toward us, then, without reason, retreat.
She is everything I know, everything I believe.

Are we afraid, then? Yes, we are afraid.
Here is friendship, or half a ton of wilderness.

Maybe it's normal to fear the thing you belong to.
But I love her. I've always loved her.

Do you love me, red mare, I want to ask, but I know
there is too much danger in it.

She flicks an ear toward me, bows her head.
Now, I tell her. *Stop*.

ii.

The red mare has learned to check my pockets
for peppermints that have slipped their cellophane.

Because she had once learned abuse, it took eighteen months
to teach her that when I lift my hand, it is to stroke her.

When I greet her, she puts her nose against mine so that we breathe
the same air, her way of saying she believes me.

She exhales warmth, honey, oats, green earth,
and I don't know what she smells on my jacket,

but I hope it's cinnamon, linen, coffee, salt,
the contentedness that lingers from lazy afternoons.

I can't help thinking that an animal that trusts
like this would be too easy for someone to harm again.

The mare tenses in the middle of our ritual—
Is it something I've done? Have I wavered?

Has my heart hardened? Has she learned that I can lie?
But she is looking at a flock of meadowlarks

cast in darkness, flying over the ground.
They have come between us and the sun.

This is an ordinary happening, but it's also spectacular
that fragile birds could punch their shapes

through such a relentlessness of light,
as if their shadows betray a greater strength:

that those small bodies can carry the weight
of a dangerous radiance.

It's only songbirds, I tell the mare. I don't tell her
that there is no courage unless fear comes first,

that this blistering brilliance means nothing at all,
except that we are alive.

iii.

   Red mare, will you follow me
   through the splintering gray gate,
   past the end of the fence line
   where the grasses thrust ochre heads
   of wild grain toward the sun?

   There are no thistles here,
   no locoweed or yuccas.
   No poison, nothing
   to draw your blood.
   The bad plants have all been pulled up
   by the roots.
   Finally, there is one
   safe place on this earth.

   For a little while, that is,
   it will be safe.
   Red mare, will you let me
   sit here quietly as you crop the grass?
   I wish I needed as little as you do.
   I wish I knew your sort of happiness.

   Are you happy?
   What if I slipped the halter off
   and you weren't tied to me, what then?
   If you could forget human language,
   would you?

If you could find water,
you could make a life for yourself
away from the world's fear,
where I must make my home.

What would you do,
red mare,
with such freedom?

Trespasses

We know what it is to care for a poor country;
eroded by the wind to tables of rock,
gopher-holed, overgrazed and overgrown
with tumbleweed and thistle,
it spreads from fence line to fence line with injury.

We stretch the barbless wire to keep it tight
on T-posts that blush with rust under flaked paint.
Try living here without breaking some skin
between yucca needle and scorpion sting.
You see how we have learned to lean in.
The wind makes us as slant as the trees.

The neighbors' dog attacks my gentle old dun,
and I shout while the pony kicks and strikes
against teeth that gnaw as if his body is already meat.
Now the dog's misfortune is something I imagine.

When I groom my glossy young gelding,
I pull prickly pear spines from his fetlocks,
and blood drips into the dust while I saddle him,
one drop at a time, almost unnoticeable,
the surest way to emptiness.
It sounds like: *Not yet. Not yet. Not yet.*

He doesn't flinch.
A horse, insensible to red, must not fathom
the depths of its wounds.

Sometimes at dusk, there is a barn owl
that watches from the fork of a crooked tree
like the ghost of a girl. No,

I never said I knew how to protect what is mine,
only how to contain it.

They Call This Weather a *Land Hurricane*

They warn us not to leave our houses,
but it's already too late to abandon the rooms
filling now with sifted dust, even if we wanted to leave;

the dry wind barrels against the doors,
the highways are barricaded by trailers blown on their sides,
downed power poles block the neighborhoods

with lines as wide as the boundaries of a country.
We watch the fences sway and bend against the gusts
as if the wood has grown green and supple again,

as if the hearts of the planks have returned to treehood,
remembering when they sweetened in a shaded forest
and sang to each other of love and weather

as their roots clasped beneath the steady earth.
When our toes touch under the blanket
it is also a miracle of love and weather—

We are together, we tell each other,
and good thing, too, because the world is getting worse.
In the darkness, the attic aches and cries.

Gray birds break fish-thin bones on the windows
and fall against the house for coyotes to find.
The next day seems like the headachy morning

after a night of uneasy dreams. Fires
sweep toward us across the trembling grass.
The wind that bruises our ribs scours the land lonely

as an empty house. Burns it like any straw body.
Watching, we forget our ages. We forget who we are.
Disaster always makes a stranger of our home,

makes it something we lose and then find again.
Something we must map.
Oh! I remember why we are here.
We are standing where we buried our tendernesses.

We Say Everything Will Be Okay

At night, we listen to the horses running
across the damp black ground
while we wait for sleep.
It's the coolness that excites them,
after the keen sun has burned their shadows
into the rocks those long bright hours.

We carry them into our dreams with us.
They carry our fear in their teeth,
not on their backs, as you might expect,
but in lines of another animal's hide in our hands.
They carry their own fear under their ribs
where we nudge it with our heels.
In our absence, such wilderness;
they are lost and returned, lost and returned to it.

When we wake, we make sure that the horses
haven't disappeared for the last time yet.
There they are again, grazing against the rising sun
while the dew wets their fetlocks.
They don't look like animals
that have flown over the dark earth
while we lay covered and silent in sleep.

Some days I can't help but wonder
if we will still be here tomorrow.

Some days, the mornings flaunt their light.
And how the blackbirds shine then,
like empty bottles someone has left
half-buried in the grass.

When Only Sage Is Left

Horses walk in a cone of blindness
that starts just past their foreheads

and goes out straight behind them,
leaving a wake of vanishing light.

When you walk behind them,
they see you disappear

on one side and reappear
suddenly on the other.

In that moment, you are like any other predator
dropping quietly from a tree

or coming up from the parting grass,
baring your teeth.

A kick betrays generations of instinct
that can never be bred out.

The mustangs browsing on the sparse grass
drag their shadows over the ravines,

grown heavy with our stories.
They could survive without us

had we not fenced them off of water,
given their grazing to cattle's many stomachs.

When only sage is left,
it will ball in their bellies like string.

To walk behind a horse, you must tell it
that the ghost in its shadow is you.

You must place your hand on its rump
on one side, and while talking to the horse,

walk to the other, so that it can
accommodate your good intentions.

See? The horse's darkness is really no different
than your darkness.

You walk into a space that shows more of its shape
the farther you move through it.

This bright land will close
behind you as you leave.

Trimmings

The flowerbed fills
with the untidiness of sleep,

ache of long dried stems
spread out like spiders' legs

and choking the beds with detritus.
Where the greens and golds

were woven into crowns of summer,
naked branches tangle

open to the sharpening sleet.
There are different birds now,

winter birds with softer songs.
Among the pebbles and twigs

the carapaces of beetles are scattered
green and dull as sea glass.

The furred seeds of the Russian sage
lie thick as down and silver.

Lives which are full and flowering
always leave too much behind.

Somehow I forget, every year,
that spring is an empty basket.

That we must weave it out of sticks.

Chore

After ten years of weather, a house
will start to fall apart.
Nails pull out of plywood. The wind
flaps the trim that used to fit flush.
The backyard gate no longer opens
when there has been a rain.
Water corrodes the fittings of the pipes,
sticks the shutoff valves unclosed.
Cracks inch up the drywall at the corners,

cracks web the grout between the bricks,
cracks spread in the concrete foundation
that seemed, at first, as if it'd last forever,
it was so smooth and thick and gray.
It was perfect. But the earth moves,
and the house, no matter how steady
its intentions, must move with it.

It is hard not to think of this
as she carries the spackle and paint
through the house, covering its scars.

Hard not to think, too, of her first house,
its small bathroom window broken out
and left in shards by some neighbor's kid
before she had moved in,

the cold beige bathtub underneath the window
cradling like a welcome gift
the dirty glass and dead hairless pink mice
with their unopened purple eyes,
as if sight would come from a bruise.
The dustpan's insufficiency then.
The globe willow weeping sap in the poor yard.

The paint conceals years as she goes.
She doesn't think of what has happened to the house
as damage. It is only the house
starting to become what it will always be.
The earth is one inexplicable round stone
shimmering with dew, despite the darkness.
Leaning through that silent darkness
almost imperceptibly toward the moon.

Cadillac Ranch

Here, graffiti isn't vandalism.
Everyone passing through can leave a mark.
I have done it. People I love have, too.
And so—it must be true—
have some of my enemies.
The decades of paint are inches thick.

It's the only monument
in this treeless prairie,
those dark shapes of cars
standing against night sky,
outlined by the glow of a lonely city
with a nuclear weapon heart.
The cars, star-voids, tipped into the ground
and leaning with the wind
the way anyone who lives here long enough
learns to do.

The cows, which graze
between the rusting bodies at night,
nose the litter of empty spray cans
with a vague remembrance
that we were there,
then left with the light.

Sometimes I want to pretend I don't know
that other names will bury ours.

Sometimes I imagine that the lines of people there
rubbing the overspray from their fingers
are counting the many ways to be alive.

The Moon (Again)

I have pulled myself in-
to this trap of sameness,
made one thing all around,
wrapped my rocky center with more rock
until I measured equally across all sides.
I know the same dark season hour after hour,
the same whirl of pigweed and ocean and smoke,
the same unholy quiet, never amended,
because sound
cannot be born in emptiness.
I've lodged around this blue stone so long
I've worn my edges off

like seaglass
which, even held to a window,
only says part of the truth
of where it came from.
The unyielding light drapes its brightness
on one side of me;
it is warm at least.
(If this life is inevitable,
at least let it be warm.)
My name... I barely remember
my name, the one I gave long ago to myself.
Too many others have named me.

I see everything from this height.
The white terrier trotting down a shadow-dappled sidewalk.
The downy baby gazing in wonder at the ceiling fan
that circles in shadowed blades on the rug.
The amber dragonflies mating among the reeds.

I am stuck as fast as the smallest soul is.
If it were otherwise, who would ever stay?
Imagine the relief of a tired orb weaver
unhitching her glistening thread
from the yellow-leafed branches,
unraveling all that she had so carefully woven—
releasing her fat summer of homes to the ground,
one by one. Releasing the dusty dead moths

back to blood and wing.
All of her mistakes, undoing themselves.
Going back through her childhood
in the filamented air, then
back to the torn cloth sack her mother left her in.

Back even before she wanted or waited for anything,
when she had no debts or attachments.

Back before the world, a place that was never hers to keep,
had been broken in two
the way it always has been:
one part with, and the other without.

Yes, some of the ache, perhaps, would be undone.
The rest of it could only become a different,
less knowable ache.

Salvage List

I take the rattling box of jars from its place
in the alder cabinet over the washing machine,
blow the dust off the metal lids,
pop the centers with my fingers
sealed/unsealed, sealed/unsealed
but the lids are screwed shut, closed fast
and the glass inside the jars is clean,
contains no trace of me, has touched no air
since the lids were machine tightened.
Has touched nothing I have touched.
What kind of hope are you bringing here?
The diamond-embossed glass sides don't speak,
resist my thumb. These vessels hold nothing yet
but the breath that they were born in.

I need each one. There was a bumper crop
of prickly pear fruit this year,
each pale green pad laden
with its deep pink flares of sweetness at the edges,
covered in tiny spines that will drive anyone to misery
if brushed against.
Imagine, rows of barbs in your skin
too tiny to see, shivers of pain
you can never be sure you've gotten rid of.
(Or did you only ever imagine it to begin with,
that enduring hurt?)

Wearing leather gloves, I have picked the fruit,
taken the stainless steel kitchen tongs and cupped it
and twisted it hard at the base,
until the cactus gave up and bled viscous slime.
I skewered what I had taken and disarmed it
with fire, igniting the glochids
and fizzing them out like old inspirations.
After that, the spines were no longer dangerous.

Forgive me for the many commitments
I have been too sick to fulfill.
Instead, this house, which was once new,
I have taken to filling with glass jars.
I have filled the jars with sugar and lemon
and the yield of a life I put into the ground
when it was young, so that it could live
parallel to mine. I have salvaged
only enough of the summer to show I existed,
and to remember that,
if you carry something once
you'll always bear part of the weight of it.

See how, despite the weeping edges,
the prickly pear holds the sun and the sand
irrevocably in its green blush.
See how it displays
the hailstorm of three years' past
in dead brown circles on the older, tougher pads,
and the short brutal days of ice
around their thickened throats.

See how this kitchen fills, one more afternoon,
with the sweetness of warming fruit.

See how a scar is not the only way
to prove there was a wound.

The End of Growing Season

The day finally arrives on which
we withdraw our protection from the garden
and abandon it to its own defenses.

It has overcome the dangerous summer:
squash bugs, drought, hail, the spreading blight.
The wearied cucumber vines are brown now,
and the tomato flowers begin to wilt, forgetting
their red intentions.

Soon the trees will become threadbare scaffolds of sky
that reflect the direction of prevailing winds
as surely as our feet show now the shape
of the shoes we wore when we were children.
Things must grow to accommodate
the caprices of a place.

Every growing season, we are reminded
that it does no good to say
that we were wronged.

Now there is nothing left that can be harmed.
For a while then, rest,
and let the cruel weather do what it will.
Though it looks like giving up,
this is not giving up.

Next year, we say,
spreading the mulch over soil
that needs refreshing,
turning down page corners
in the seed catalogues,
drawing maps of raised beds and trellises
in lined yellow pads.

Oh, next year.

In Early Fall

The angle is just right. The midmorning light
makes the windows shine from across the street
and brightens the curves of bottles on the shelves.

We are still new-enough awakened from darkness
that we are relieved to realize the growing warmth,
the way every blade of grass is highlighted

so that the deer are no longer ghosts slipping through a gray field
but bright beasts that cross the road, then turn to watch us pass.
The coyote that laughed like a lost fiend last night

has gone, and the pasture sparkles with gold tips.
The garden, somehow, is still producing its little bit,
and we have brought the last tomatoes in
and set them onto the sill to ripen.

The mason jars standing in rows along the sink
cast the light of their figures across the kitchen.
To look at them, you'd think they could preserve
even this day, even now.

ACKNOWLEDGMENTS

Atticus Review, "Trace Elements"

Baltimore Review, "Ghazal After the Electrocardiogram" and "These Habits"

Cordite Poetry Review, "It Gets Easier"

Delta River Review, "Imago" and "Paradise"

Diode, "The Fall of Rome" and "How to Get a Hoya to Bloom"

Glass Poetry Press: Poets Resist, "Texas Strong"

The Heartland Review, "Dear Disease"

The Penn Review, "They Call This Weather a *Land Hurricane*"

Pleiades, "An Abecedarian for Barrenness"

Poets Reading the News, "Cadillac Ranch" (as "Other Names")

Rattle: Poets Respond, "Anything Worth Saving" and "The Moon of a Moon
    is a Moonmoon"

Ruminate, "Land Management"

San Pedro River Review, "Locoweed," "Trimmings," and "Trespasses"

The Southern Review, "When the Cottontail Doesn't Return"

Taos Journal of Poetry, "Mustang"

The Texas Observer, "In Early Fall"

THRUSH, "When Only Sage is Left"

CHERA HAMMONS is the recipient of poetry awards through PEN Texas and the Texas Institute of Letters. She holds an MFA from Goddard College. Her work, which is rooted in love for the natural world, appears in *Baltimore Review*, *Pleiades*, *Poetry*, *Rattle*, *The Southern Review*, *The Sun*, *The Texas Observer*, and elsewhere. She lives on the windswept prairies of the Texas Panhandle. Her newest poetry collection, *Birds of America*, is forthcoming through The Dial Press, an imprint of Penguin Random House, in 2026.

Belle Point Press is a literary small press along the Arkansas-Oklahoma border. Our mission is simple: Stick around and read. Learn more at bellepointpress.com.